Popular Garden Birds

by Joe Firmin

W. Foulsham & Co. Ltd.
London · New York · Toronto · Cape Town · Sydney

W. FOULSHAM & COMPANY LTD
Yeovil Road, Slough, Berkshire SL1 4JH

ISBN 0-572-01445-7

Printed in Great Britain by
St Edmundsbury Press Ltd, Bury St Edmunds, Suffolk

Contents

Introduction

In these days of increased leisure and a growing interest in the garden as a place for relaxation and pleasure, many people want to make their gardens attractive to birds.

There is a boom in the feeding of birds in the garden during those months of the year when there is only a minimum of natural food. Most people with gardens are also interested in providing nest boxes and natural cover suitable for nesting.

The aim of this book is to help you create a miniature bird sanctuary in your garden. A place where you can provide food, shelter and nest sites, both man-made and natural. There are suggestions on the most suitable trees, shrubs and herbaceous perennial plants which offer birds cover and food in season.

Bird tables, bird feeders and nest boxes can give you endless pleasure from watching the lively behaviour and colourful plumage of the surprisingly large variety of birds which visit even the smallest gardens. And the gardener who sets out to attract and protect birds is playing a part in the conservation of our precious wildlife.

The book contains plenty of information on the practical ways of encouraging birds to the garden and on some of the snags which should be avoided when putting up and supplying a bird table and food containers.

Chapter One

How to Attract Birds to Your Garden

The fundamental requirements for attracting birds to your garden, whatever its size, are shelter and protection; convenient nest sites; water at all seasons, particularly in times of drought or hard frost; and regular supplies of food, bearing in mind the needs of particular bird species and individual tastes. Birds appreciate a change of diet as much as you do.

The best way to protect and attract birds is to provide them with natural cover, and I will deal with planning and planting to achieve this in Chapter 7.

An adequate supply of water is one of the most important points to bear in mind when you are establishing your garden bird sanctuary. No garden which lacks this facility will attract bird life; drinking water is essential, and places for bathing and preening are equally vital (see Chapter 2).

A well-kept lawn or area of turf is important. There you can easily see birds through your windows as they hunt for worms, beetle grubs and ants. I never tire of watching blackbirds, thrushes and robins as they listen and look with heads turned to one side, then pounce on their hidden prey and pull it out of the grass. It is a remarkable example of co-ordination of acute eyesight and hearing.

It is a mistake to kill off worms in your lawns. Although they make unsightly casts, they do a most valuable job in the garden by aerating, draining and enriching the soil, and they are an important part of the daily diet of birds.

I must stress the importance of designing your layout on a number of levels to enclose little hollows, banks and sheltered nooks where birds can forage contentedly for insects and seeds out of the worst of wind and weather, and under the protection of leaves and low branches. South-facing rockeries with an irregular jumble of masonry and plants are popular with the smaller birds. There they can find many small insects, slugs, snails and woodlice among the crevices and stones or under leaves.

During the severe drought of 1976, the driest summer for more than 200 years, my own rockery was frequently visited by thrushes, blackbirds and dunnocks. They found slugs, caterpillars and insects among the cool, moist leaves of alpine plants and succulents which had not been shrivelled up by the glaring sun like most of the other vegetation in the garden.

Trees and shrubs which produce a plentiful crop of berries are vital in the bird garden. The best of these will be listed in Chapter 7. I emphasise the value of hedges in attracting a varied bird population.

In my own garden I have a long sweetbrier rose hedge which offers dense prickly cover for nesting birds. In winter greenfinches come to eat the profusion of scarlet hips. The fragrance of the sweetbrier foliage after a summer shower perfumes the whole garden – it always reminds me of the scent of ripe apples.

You must make sure that birds are protected from wind. Like us, they hate to be buffeted and frozen by icy blasts, especially in spring when the nesting season is in full swing. To cut off the winds on the north side of my garden, I have a tall hedge of *Cotoneaster lacteus*. This attractive evergreen, with its arching branches and tall growth, bears creamy-white flowers in summer and is decked with red berries in winter. Flocks of fieldfares and redwings, which come to us from Scandinavia for the cold months of the year, join the garden blackbirds and thrushes to make short work of the berries as soon as there is a nip in the air. Smaller birds hunt for insects at the base of the hedge and the screen of tough dark green leaves gives welcome protection from the worst of the wind, rain, sleet and snow.

In one corner of the garden, I have planted a clump of laurel which is kept well trimmed to ensure bushy growth. It offers dense

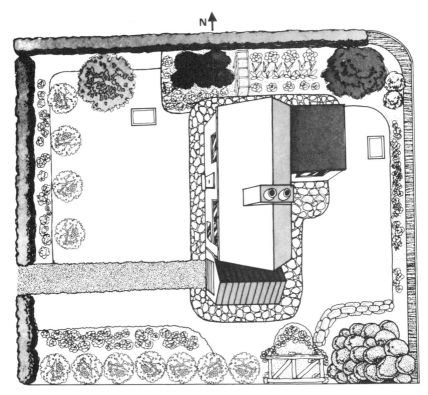

Trees and shrubs can provide shelter and nesting places as well as berries to attract birds.

cover and is tenanted in spring and summer by nesting blackbirds and thrushes. But a word of advice: don't overdo the planting of laurel, rhododendrons or azaleas. Shrubs of this kind block light from the ground, fail to attract insects, and don't provide good sites for nesting.

If you have room in the garden, fruit trees are as good for birds as they are for your household budget. Old apple and pear trees attract a great many birds, particularly tits, finches, robins and nuthatches. Greenfinches and chaffinches often like to nest in them. A friend who left an old gnarled apple tree at the bottom of his garden was rewarded with a nesting pair of nuthatches who commandeered a hole in the lichen-covered trunk. Leave some fruit on the trees in autumn and you will be certain to attract blackbirds, song and mistle thrushes, redwings and fieldfares. Mixed flocks of titmice hunt among the branches for the larvae and tiny eggs of various insects.

Go easy on the larger conifers. They grow tall and gaunt and their dense masses of needles keep out light and suppress plant growth on the ground underneath their branches. I have only a few of the more compact fastigiate (upright) varieties. These include the golden form of the yew, a couple of Irish junipers and a *Cupressus arizonica conica*, which has pretty, bluish-green foliage. Linnets and dunnocks regularly nest in them. The fleshy red berries of yew are favourite food of thrushes, blackbirds and starlings. The birds eat the pulp but pass out the poisonous seeds without suffering any harm. Remember that yew bark and needles are poisonous.

Holly is excellent in every way. Well-grown trees or bushes give shelter and roosting places and the berries are eaten by the thrush tribe. But don't forget that hollies are either male or female; only the female tree produces the berries, and you must have a male nearby for cross-fertilisation.

One variety, *Ilex aquifolium pyramidalis* is self fertile. As its name suggests it has a close, pyramidal growth, carries an abundance of berries, and the leaves bear few spines. I have a pyramidal holly, as well as the variety Golden King (with yellow margins to the leaves and few spines) and the silver-margined form known as Silver Queen. Oddly enough Golden King is female and Silver Queen male.

The cultivated forms of barberry (berberis) are useful in the bird garden for their berries contain Vitamin C. They make good hedges with the added bonus of yellow and orange flowers in season. I have mentioned *Cotoneaster lacteus* but there are many other members of the Cotoneaster family with which I will deal more fully in Chapter 7.

Rowan trees, or mountain ash, are recommended for their big crops of glistening red, orange and yellow berries, greatly loved by thrushes. Some gardeners think of the common elder as a pest, but the bird gardener who has a wild corner should grow one or two bushes for the purple berries which are eaten greedily by many species of birds. Migrant warblers love to dally among the elder fruits on mellow autumn days.

I have plenty of honeysuckles along my fences. They bunch up to give thick cover for nests and their luscious berries are eaten by blackbirds, tits, bullfinches and warblers. Ivy is also useful for attracting birds to walls and fences. The thrush family eat the dark berries, while wrens and other small birds like the cover of the evergreen leaves. Old ivy clumps are favourite nest sites for pied wagtails and spotted flycatchers.

Viburnums and spindles should be planted for their berries and the vivid colour of their autumn leaves. Another bush I keep for its berries as well as its flowers is the so-called Himalayan Honeysuckle *(Leycesteria formosa)*. Birds adore the fleshy purple berries.

The yellow-berried *Pyracantha rogersiana* against my front wall gets stripped of its fruit by thrushes and blackbirds – but only after they have first raided the red-berried pyracanthas. The same is true of the yellow-berried rowan called Joseph Rock.

I find that my Oregon thornless blackberry, trained against a fence, attracts warblers and finches in late summer when there is a huge crop of berries. Sometimes little family parties of bullfinches, piping plaintively to each other, come to peck at the ripe fruit.

Some annual and perennial plants grown in the flower garden bear seeds which birds like to eat. I grew up on an Essex nursery where many flower-seed crops were grown and I remember with pleasure the tinkling flocks of goldfinches which used to raid the seeding heads of French and African marigolds, godetia and cornflower. All these flowers are easy to grow in the garden. If you leave the seed heads on the plants as long as possible, you are likely to attract many finches to the garden.

It is a very good plan to grow some sunflowers. Not only are these stately plants good to look at, but greenfinches find their seeds irresistible. Finches also like the seeds of gaillardia, cosmos, linum (flax), sweet sultan and summer chrysanthemum. I notice that bullfinches are fond of the seeds of delphinium, antirrhinum, larkspur and pansy, as well as the berries of privet and rowan.

As a great deal of your birdwatching will be done from the house, you should provide the birds with a selection of perching posts and singing posts, so placed as to give you an uninterrupted view. It is a good plan to put up a T-shaped perch made from a rustic pole about two metres high with a short transverse section on top – if possible near a drinking pool or bird bath. The birds will use it as a staging point before they go down to drink and bathe.

Male blackbirds love to sit on such a perch to sing out to all the world that the surroundings are their special territory. If you are fortunate enough to have a pair of spotted flycatchers in your garden during the summer, you will find that they use the perch as a base for their acrobatic flights to capture passing insects.

During the winter, birds must spend 16 hours a day at roost. They lose a lot of body heat and therefore choose a place out of the wind and rain. They need the cover of evergreens or thickets and you must always think of this aspect when laying out the bird garden. It is best to have a variety of compact evergreens grown in clumps. Thick ivy, grown on a south-facing wall or fence, is much used by roosting birds. Close-foliaged conifers, such as some of the upright cypresses, are often chosen by dunnocks, robins, finches and sparrows for roosting. Fir trees, with a more open growing habit, do not offer such a dense cover or such good protection from wind and weather.

A T-shaped perch will encourage many bird visitors, especially if it is near a drinking pool or bird bath.

Chapter Two

Foods and Feeding Habits

We now consider the feeding preferences of birds and the means of providing them with water throughout the year. In Chapter 4 I will describe bird tables and various devices which can be bought or made to contain food.

Before you start to think about supplying the birds with food, take a close look at the bills of species in your garden. They will indicate feeding habits and foods. Finches and sparrows have strong, stubby bills adapted to crush seeds and grain. Robins, wrens, dunnocks and warblers have slender bills which they use for feeding on insects and other small, soft-bodied creatures.

As you would expect, the best foods for birds are those they would normally find in the countryside. If you plant your garden with a mixture of trees and shrubs which produce edible berries and fruits, and herbaceous plants with nutritious seeds, you have gone a long way towards ensuring food for the birds in autumn and winter. You can supplement these supplies by going into the countryside in late summer and autumn to gather berries from the rowan, elder and hawthorn, crab apples, hazel nuts, beech nuts (mast) and acorns. If they are first dried and then stored (with nuts and acorns) in a warm place out of strong light, the berries will keep for a long time. Don't stack fruits on trays in such a way that they bruise, or they will also rot. Gather fir, pine and larch cones and take out the seeds from their scales.

I make a point of picking the seed heads of wild plants such as dock, thistle, stinging nettle, knapweed, teazle and ragwort and hang

Hawfinch   *Great Tit*

Birds' bills are a good indication of the feeding habits of the species.

Song Thrush

Woodpecker

Nuthatch

Robin

them up in muslin bags. I shake or beat out the dry, clean seeds when they are needed for the bird table. You should also add the seeds of garden plants to packeted seed mixtures and wild seeds. Sometimes seed merchants and farmers will sell you bags of the cleanings from their machines, which contain a mixture of weed seeds and grain, but first make sure that anything of this kind is absolutely free from chemical dressings or pollutants.

Kitchen scraps should be saved for the birds. Bread is the commonest waste, and wholemeal is better than the soggy product which nowadays passes for white bread. Uncooked pastry is often preferred to bread and can be moulded into shapes to fit a corner of the bird table or feeding tray.

Potatoes, particularly if baked in their jackets, are popular and stale cake is also eagerly eaten. Make sure that cake and similar foods are not put on the bird table in wet weather, otherwise they will soon be reduced to a soggy, inedible mess. Don't put out bread when nestlings are being fed in spring and summer. Minced raw meat, cooked and chopped bacon rinds, cheese and bone marrow are all good. You can use these ingredients to make a pudding for the birds: put seeds, peanuts, oatmeal, cheese, dry cake and other scraps in a container and cover the mixture with hot fat (weigh the mixture and use half its weight of melted fat). Put the pudding on the bird table when the fat has hardened. Avoid all salty and spicy foods when you are making up a mixture of scraps.

Apart from using fat to bind bird puddings or in mixtures of household scraps, you can put it in meshed containers (details of which are given in Chapter 4). Bacon rind can be hung up in strips on a wire or stout cord. Tits love lumps of raw beef suet on which they can swing as they pick off lumps. I also use a device called a suet stick. This is a short length of silver birch log into which a number of holes 2.5 cm (1 in.) deep have been bored; when the holes are stuffed with suet the gadget provides hours of entertainment for the birdwatcher as well as food for tits, woodpeckers and nuthatches. Nuthatches and woodpeckers also like to hammer with their bills at the kernels of almonds and brazil nuts wedged in the crevices of posts or trellises.

Home-made mixtures of bird food can be used from autumn as soon as temperatures fall sharply and supplies of natural foods begin to decline. Regular feeding should be stopped as soon as the weather warms up in March or early April. By then there is an increasing amount of insect life and other natural foods, and birds will be disinclined to visit the bird table. Remember, too, that some foods offered on bird tables and in containers can be harmful if fed to young nestlings. Peanuts cannot be properly digested by nestling tits even though their parents eat and enjoy the nuts.

Recent springs have been late and cold so the time for stopping supplies of home-made and proprietary bird foods must be a matter of commonsense, taking into account the prevailing weather conditions. As soon as there is consistently warm weather, stop feeding.

As a general rule home-made mixtures are most valuable when the harder weather sets in at the end of the year and throughout the bleak months of January and February. This is the vital time for bird survival.

There are several brands of packeted wild bird foods on the market. The best of these have been specially formulated to satisfy the appetites and nutritional needs of a wide variety of birds. The only snag is that they are expensive when you need a lot during the winter months. You can supplement proprietary mixtures by buying crushed hemp, linseed, canary seed, millet, maize, buckwheat, oats and corn. Always use oatmeal in a dry state; porridge is far too sticky and wet. If you are putting out rice, however, it should be cooked. Try to prevent it from getting too congealed.

Almost any kind of nut is good for the birds. Peanuts are the first choice, rich in calories and easy to handle and store. If you don't remove the shells you can string some on stout thread to hang from the bird table or a branch. Tits and nuthatches adore swinging on these peanut strings.

Peanut strings attract tits and nuthatches.

I have already mentioned that nuthatches are fond of brazil nuts. You can shell some and hang them up, or distribute pieces on the bird table. Coconut is popular. Saw a shell in half and suspend the pieces upside down so that rain can't get in. Never offer desiccated or ground coconut – it swells up in birds' stomachs with disastrous results. Discontinue feeding nuts and all high protein foods during the nesting season. There is enough natural food at this time of year. Peanuts cannot be digested by nestling tits, and any kind of sticky or over-soft food is bad.

Mealworms are the best kind of live food but you can also offer ants' eggs (actually pupae, not eggs, of ants) and gentles (fly grubs). You can buy gentles from fishing tackle and bait shops. Personally I don't use them as I much prefer mealworms. Gentles are bad for nestlings.

You can buy supplies of mealworms, the larvae of a small black beetle, from pet shops and put them out on the bird table or a ledge in a glazed china dish. Robins are crazy about them and you can easily tame one to come and take them from your hand. If you want to try your hand at producing your own mealworms, buy about three hundred from a pet shop and put them in a large biscuit tin with ventilation holes punched in the lid. The bottom of the tin should be covered with a layer of hessian, sprinkled with pieces of wholemeal bread, bran and pieces of raw potato. Add two more layers like the first. The mealworms go in and out of the hessian and eat the food. After a few weeks, they turn into pupae from which adult beetles eventually emerge. These pair and produce eggs, renewing the supply of mealworms. You can gather ants' eggs from wild nests or buy them from pet shops or dealers in aquaria.

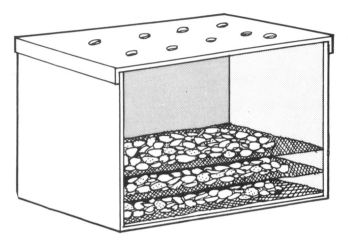

It is easy to produce your own mealworms in a specially adapted biscuit tin.

Birds need water both for drinking and to keep their plumage in top condition. After a bath, a bird rubs its feathers with oil collected from the preen gland above its tail.

Unless you are lucky enough to have a pond or stream in the garden, you must turn your attention to supplying water for the birds. You can buy bird baths, but the best are expensive. A simple, cheap alternative is to use an upturned dustbin lid, either sunk in the ground or supported on three bricks. The depth of water should not be more than 10.2 cm (4 in). Make sure it is clean and free from any pollutants.

If you have time, you can look round junk shops or attend auctions for one of those solidly-made Victorian metal saucer baths which are easy to convert into a small pond or large bird bath. Sunk into the ground in a partly-shaped spot, with a layer of fine sand in the bottom, it can be planted with water weeds, rushes and water lilies.

A gardener-handyman might make a cement pond holding not less than 60 litres (13 gallons) of water. One end should be shallow. Small birds like a depth of about 3 centimetres so make sure there is a gentle slope. Don't site the pond too close to any shrubbery which may conceal a cat or other predator.

You can prevent the bird bath from freezing by using an aquarium immersion heater covered with gravel. If it is connected to a submerged thermostat it will prevent a freeze-up. Make sure the mains lead is of outdoor quality and check all fittings to ensure your own safety, and that of the birds. You can put a slow-burning night lamp underneath a bird bath raised above ground, but never use glycerine or other anti-freeze additives. They are injurious to birds' plumage.

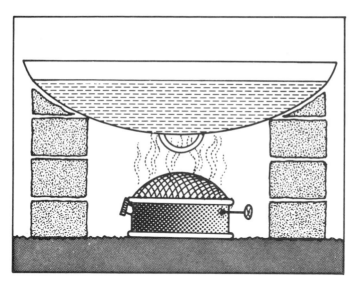

A slow-burning night lamp can be used to prevent a raised bird bath from freezing.

Chapter Three

Nesting Sites and Nest Boxes

If you are to make a real success of attracting birds to your garden, you must provide plenty of natural and artificial nest sites. In the last chapter I described shrubs, trees and hedges suitable for nesting. It is worth reiterating that you can improve hedge cover by careful pruning below a height of two metres. All pruning should be done in early spring and autumn, and hedges and trees left undisturbed during the breeding season.

You can help nest-building operations by leaving out in the garden some of the materials gathered by birds for nest construction. They are sharp-eyed and quickly pick up anything of use. I remember one pair of mistle thrushes which used torn-up shreds of a football match programme, and a chaffinch nest colourfully ornamented with pieces of confetti.

Assemble pieces of sheep's wool gathered from barbed wire fences; small soft feathers or down; dried grasses and thin straw; combings of human hair and animal fur; dry leaves of oak and beech; short pieces of cotton; and rootlets dried out after digging the garden. Tuck the hair and wool into a cleft in a fence. Other material can be suspended from a tree branch in a large mesh bag through which the birds can pull what they want. Avoid messy piles which can blow about in your own and neighbouring gardens.

Many of the birds in gardens nest in holes. Before dealing with nest boxes and how to make them, we should first think about natural holes which tits, tree sparrows, nuthatches and woodpeckers can use. You may already have some old trees with holes in the decaying wood, but you can sometimes start some of your own with the help of a brace and bit. If you drill a few holes in an old branch or trunk, a woodpecker may finish off the excavations.

Wherever possible, do not fell trees that have holes or fill the cavities in walls and fences. If you are building a garden wall, leave some gaps suitable for pied wagtails, tits, spotted flycatchers and robins.

A lean-to or open garden shed is a wonderful haven for birds. Leave faggots and bundles of peasticks against the side of the shed for nesting blackbirds, dunnocks and wrens. Rolls of wire netting also attract wrens and blackbirds. The shelves and ledges inside an open shed provide homes for swallows, blackbirds and robins. One year a pair of robins nested in the sagging pocket of an old gardening coat hung up on a nail, and a friend with a dilapidated greenhouse potting shed was amused to find that robins had built on the floor of an old bird cage without a door, which had been propped up in a corner.

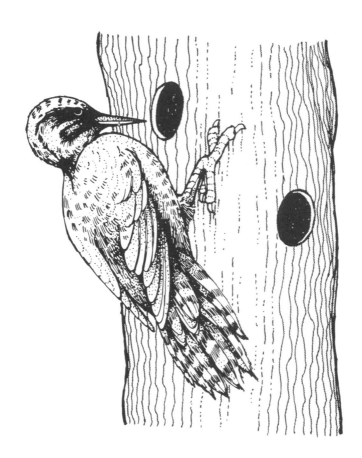

A woodpecker may be attracted to nest if you drill a few holes in an old branch or trunk.

Robins, wrens and spotted flycatchers will build inside old kettles and cans wedged in trees, or in ivy on a wall. Make sure that the spout of a kettle points downwards so that no water gathers inside. Place all such containers well clear of the ground and shaded from direct sunshine.

To encourage tree creepers, nail pieces of virgin cork, or large sections of bark to a tree at such an angle that the little birds can build in the gap between the bark or cork and the trunk. There is also available a wedge-shaped nest box which can be bought specially for tree creepers.

Wrens will make use of sacking to support their finely-woven domed nests. You can help them by folding a stout piece of hessian and nailing it to the underside of a bough or leaning tree trunk two or three metres from the ground. You can also put sacking under the eaves of a shed or garage. The idea is to create a fold or tunnel in which the wrens can build.

Wrens will use any available nest site – an old kettle wedged in a hedge is ideal.

House martins construct their cupped mud nests under the eaves and gables of houses, but many of them are taken over by aggressive house sparrows. You can buy artificial nest cups made from a plastic material from Nerine Nurseries or the RSPB (see page 94). These keep out sparrows and encourage other martins to build their own nests alongside. They are held in position by hooks so that you can slide them out to inspect the interiors. The entrance hole for martins' nest cups should be no more than 2 cm (¾ in.) deep to keep out sparrows. You can also deter sparrows from usurping martin nests by hanging from the guttering a series of small weights, on pieces of string about 30 cm (12 in.) long and 10 cm (4 in.) apart. Martins can approach nests at a much steeper angle than the sparrows, avoiding the hanging cords.

Nest boxes are of two main designs: an enclosed box type with a small entrance hole, and trays or ledges with or without sides. The open-front model is good for robins, wrens and flycatchers, and a box with open front and sides is popular with blackbirds and thrushes. There are also boxes and trays suitable for nesting owls and kestrels, but these are of interest only to those who have large gardens or areas of woodland.

You can buy nest boxes of several types at reasonable prices from the Royal Society for the Protection of Birds (see page 94). If you ask for information, the Society will send you literature on making the best use of nest boxes and all kinds of bird furniture.

18

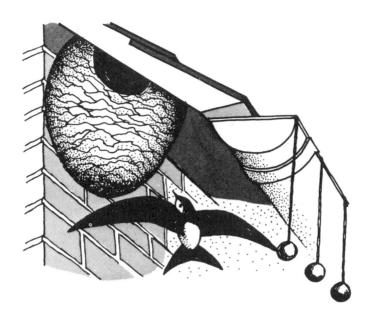

Hanging small weights on cords from the guttering will deter sparrows from using martins' nests.

Other suppliers of well-made nest boxes are listed on page 94.

If you are sufficiently handy, you will probably find it enjoyable to make your own nest boxes and other bird furniture. It is not a difficult task for the practised do-it-yourself enthusiast. The British Trust for Ornithology (see page 94) produce a *Nestboxes* guide, No. 2 by Chris de Feu.

The standard nest box for smaller hole-nesting birds such as tits, wrens, redstarts, tree sparrows and nuthatches should be made from wood not less than 2 cm (¾ in.) thick. Choose a hard wood if possible, but cedar is the best of the soft woods and weathers well. Sometimes you can get some planks of secondhand floor boarding.

To make the box, take a plank 136 cm (54 in.) long by 15 cm (6 in.) wide and cut lengths off it as follows; roof 21 cm (8½ in.); back 30 cm (12 in.); front 18 cm (7 in.) and floor 19 cm (7½ in.). This will leave you with a section 48 cm (19 in.) long for the sides. Using a pencil and ruler, mark a point 30 cm (12 in.) along one edge of the plank; still measuring from the same end, make a mark 18 cm (7 in.) along the other edge; join the marks with a diagonal line across the width of the plank and cut along it. When the box is assembled, these side pieces will support a sloping roof which has a slight overhang. Fix the joints with screws or oval nails, using a sealing compound before you nail or screw them into final position. The nest box must be snugly fitting and completely rainproof. A coat of creosote will help to preserve the wood.

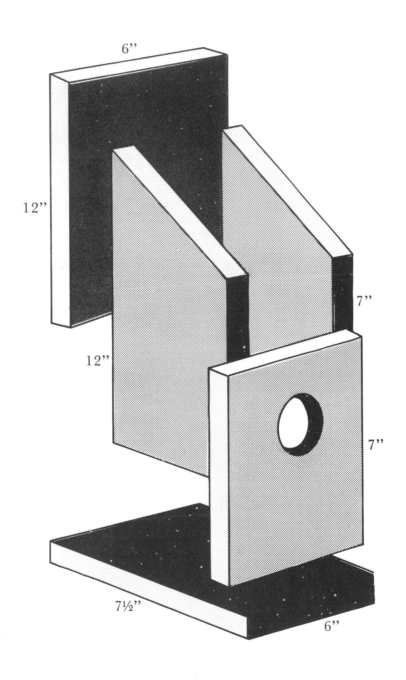

6"

12"

12"

7"

7"

7½"

6"

A nesting box for small birds can be made from old floor boarding.

Attach a wooden batten about 10 cm (4 in.) wide to the back of the nest box for fixing to trees or walls, and cut an entry hole 3 cm (1³⁄₁₆ in.) in diameter either on the side or the front of the box. The hole must be high up on the box, not less than 12 cm (4¾ in.) from the floor. To prevent the hole from being enlarged by squirrels and woodpeckers, you can front the box with metal, pierced with a matching hole. (The RSPB supplies these with some of their nestboxes.) It is essential to bore a hole for drainage and ventilation in the floor of the box. The lid should be hinged with rustless metal or strips of plastic or leather. Some people prefer to secure the lid with screws.

A metal hole cover will stop squirrels or woodpeckers enlarging a nest box hole.

Nest boxes should be fixed at a height of two metres or more on tree trunks, walls or posts in October and November. Tilt them slightly so they do not collect rain water through the entry hole. Make sure the boxes are well out of the reach of cats, rats and grey squirrels. They must be in positions where they neither freeze in cold winds, nor grill for hours in the hot sun. The best sites face north or north east. Avoid a landing perch, as this could help predators. Take care when fixing the boxes to trees – if you consider screws or nails may damage bark, then fasten the box with leather or webbing straps.

When the young have flown, clean the box and give it a dose of pyrethrum-based insecticide. Never use DDT or other persistent chemicals. Open-plan nest boxes should be placed in the forks of trees and ivy-clad places where they can attract spotted flycatchers, pied wagtails and robins.

A north or north-east facing sight is best for a nesting box.

BIRDS WHICH USE NESTBOXES

E = enclosed type   OF = open-fronted or ledge type

Tawny Owl (E, 20 cm. diameter hole at top; also chimney type)
Treecreeper (E and special wedge-shaped box)

Stock Dove (E)	Redstart (E)
Great Spotted Woodpecker (E)	Robin (OF)
Green Woodpecker (E)	Spotted Flycatcher (OF)
Wryneck (E)	Pied Flycatcher (E)
Jackdaw (E and OF)	Starling (E)
Great Tit (E)	House Sparrow (E)
Blue Tit (E)	Tree Sparrow (E)
Coal Tit (E)	Wren (E)
Marsh Tit (E)	Blackbird (OF)
Nuthatch (E)	Pied Wagtail (OF)

Chapter Four

Bird Tables and Bird Furniture

The main item in the gardener's equipment for feeding birds is the bird table. It pays to devote as much time and cash as you can afford to buying or making a sturdy, weather-resistant model and siting it in the best position. The table should be placed near the cover of some shrubs or a hedge, but out of range of a leaping cat. Don't put it in the middle of a lawn where there is always the risk of interference from cats and squirrels or, in larger gardens, from owls and hawks. Birds do not feel at ease in a wide open space some distance from shelter.

Position your table carefully so that it suits both the birds and you.

Ideally, you should position your table so that birds can reach it by a series of short flights between bushes and trees, or a row of posts. The distance of the table from the house is also important. When birds are really used to you, they will take less and less notice of your watching them and come to accept you as a normal part of their everyday environment, but until you have conditioned your bird visitors to this desirable degree of confidence, it is best to place the table so that any movements made by an observer just inside a window are not easily seen. As the use of binoculars for prolonged periods of time is tiring on eyes and wrists, the aim must eventually be to have the bird table close enough to the house to dispense with optical aids, except on special occasions when a very close view is needed.

As in the case of nest boxes, you can either buy bird tables ready made or make you own. It is worth bearing in mind that the cost of wood is extremely high and not likely to come down, but if you shop around or use wood salvaged from other pieces of furniture you can cut the expense.

The Royal Society for the Protection of Birds makes and sells a standard bird table which I can strongly recommend.

You must fit your table to a smooth pole, whether it is made of metal or wood; rough-barked, rustic poles offer the perfect invitation to clambering cats and squirrels. You can fit a biscuit tin under the table as an anti-squirrel device. Place the biscuit tin on the ground, open end up and drive the pole through it. Leave the top of the tin open and no animal will climb over it.

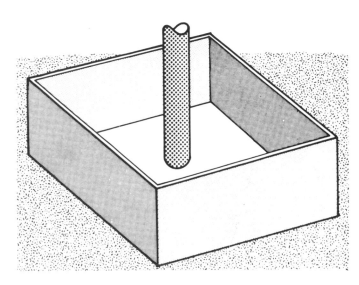

An open biscuit tin on the ground below a bird table will deter unwelcome animals.

On page 94 you will find the addresses of some reputable suppliers of garden bird equipment. All the makers on my list offer good bird tables made in different styles, but all to a single basic design. Steer clear of the curious rustic tables ornamented with all sorts of perches and roof adornments. The simpler and cleaner the table, the better it will function – and it will not attract unwelcome predators and pests.

I prefer a table with a roof. It helps to keep food dry and provides a place to hang a seed hopper. Birds like somewhere to shelter from driving rain, sleet and snow and huddle under the bird table roof in severe weather. Some people nevertheless consider a roof an unnecessary adornment and contend that it serves to attract feathered and furred enemies which lurk under its cover, or use it as a vantage point to launch attacks on the birds visiting the table. Personally, however, I think the advantages of a roof speak for themselves.

If you do decide to make your own bird table, you should not make the feeding tray too small. Mine is 45 cm (18 in.) long by 30 cm (12 in.) wide but you can go for a larger area if you wish. Commonsense dictates the size; don't get so carried away by your enthusiasm that you try to make a big, unwieldy tray which will frighten away the birds and be hard to support.

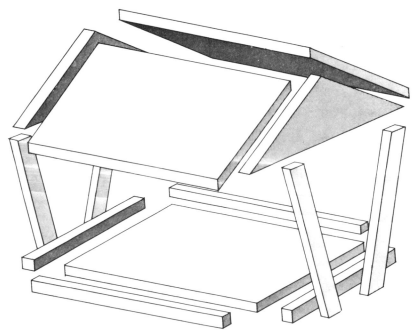

A good size for a bird table is about 45 cm (18 in.) long by 30 cm (12 in.) wide. A roof helps to keep food dry and provides shelter for the birds.

Put a lip about 3 cm (1¼ in.) high round the edge of the tray, but leave a gap for easy cleaning of the table and drainage of rain water. The lip prevents food which has been scattered on the table from being blown away by the wind or swept off by scuffling birds. Pieces of bread and other food are pushed against the ledge by birds in order to make pecking and picking up easier.

Scrap baskets which you can hang from the bird table or from branches are valuable extras. The best models, in my opinion, are those made of plastic-coated wire mesh with a lid. These will take supplies of mixed kitchen scraps and shelled peanuts.

Avoid scrap baskets made from collapsible wire mesh – small birds get their feet and legs jammed between springy wires. Never use anything which has sharp edges or points or is not strongly and safely made. Resist the temptation to buy any of the flimsy bird feeders often offered at knock-down prices in pet shops and stores. These 'bargains' can injure birds if they come apart during stormy weather. Stick to appliances made and supplied by organisations and firms which specialize in bird furniture. You may pay a bit more but it is worth the extra money to have feeders which are strong and absolutely safe.

A useful seed dispenser is one which has a see-through top section which enables the food level to be checked and were the base can be released for filling and cleaning. Spiral feeders for holding peanuts can be dangerous if they are too whippy; birds' legs may get trapped in the coils. Again, go for safe and well-tried models which have heavy-duty steel coils covered with PVC to prevent rusting.

Seed hoppers can often be used in conjunction with bird tables. They should keep seed dry in almost all weathers and slide neatly under the roof. You can, of course, supplement the mixed seeds bought from pet shops and corn merchants with wild and garden seeds you have gathered and dried during the autumn.

In the chapter on foods and feeding I stressed the value of peanuts, either shelled or unshelled. Although the cost of this staple item keeps rising, the nuts still represent good value. There are many inexpensive devices for offering peanuts. PVC-coated metal grille baskets are excellent, and I use the refillable nylon bags which are sold in pet shops. For some inexplicable reason siskins love to peck at peanuts suspended in red nylon mesh bags – why they go for red remains a mystery. Greenfinches adore peanuts and compete with the tits to swing on the baskets and bags.

If you want to put up some unshelled nuts, the best plan is to thread on a piece of thin galvanized wire about 50 cm (20 in.) long. Cut the wire off obliquely at one end to make a sharp point for skewering the nuts. Then bend the top end into a hanging hook and turn up the lower end to prevent the nuts from slipping off. When attached to the hanging point with an elastic band, the string of nuts twirls round and the birds love it. So will you as you watch their antics.

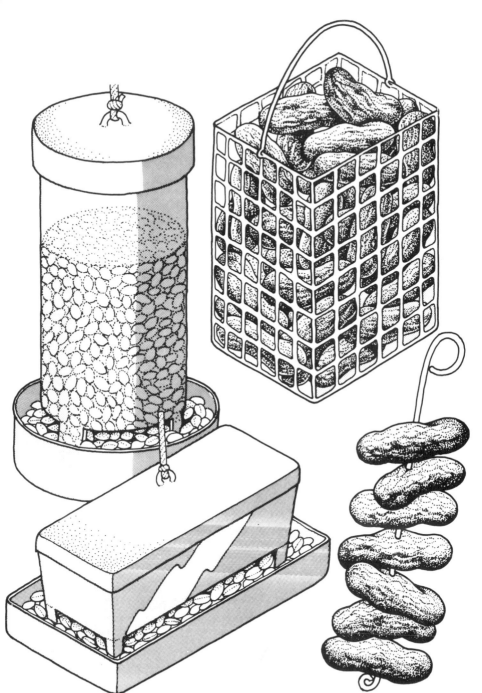

Buy seed dispensers from a reputable source such as the RSPB. PVC-coated metal grille baskets are excellent peanut dispensers, or you can thread unshelled nuts onto thin galvanized wire.

I have already mentioned the making of a suet stick. You can also make a tit bell by filling a cup-shaped container with scraps and seed bound together with hot fat. When the mixture has set, you can hang the bell upside down for tits and nuthatches to peck. Even great spotted woodpeckers are attracted to this and the suet stick, while sparrows and starlings are unable to reach the food.

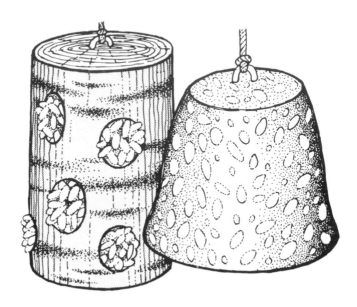

Suet sticks and tit bells are easy to make and attract tits, nuthatches and even woodpeckers.

Many birds do not like to feed at a bird table. You can cater for their needs by putting out food on an old tray or a piece of board which is left on the ground under a tree or between shrubs, though not too close to cover from which a lurking cat could pounce. Clear up uneaten food at the end of the day, otherwise you will encourage rats and mice. Dunnocks, chaffinches, yellowhammers, and even blackbirds and song thrushes, seem to prefer feeding on the ground to jostling with other birds on a table.

One of the great problems with a bird table is the dominant and aggressive behaviour of certain species, particularly starlings and house sparrows, which grab a lot of the food by sheer weight of numbers. If you try to deter the starlings by putting wire netting round the table with a mesh wide enough only to admit smaller birds, this also keeps out blackbirds and thrushes. As starlings are not on the scene so quickly in the mornings as many other species, you can try putting food out early. I try to capitalize on the fact that both starlings and sparrows are basically wary species. I offer them food in an area of the garden separate from the main feeding stations.

Wire mesh around the bird table will keep out the larger birds.

A simple bird table is suitable for the smallest of gardens.

29

Birds should be fed regularly at the same time each day. They depend on you for survival in the worst of the winter weather. Reduce the amount of high-energy foods in April, but maintain interest in the bird table by making regular small offerings of low-bulk foods throughout spring, summer and autumn.

Hanging bird tables are ideal for those with only a balcony or window ledge.

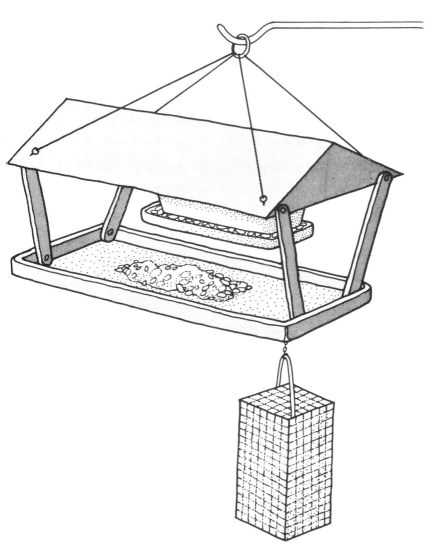

This hanging bird table fixes to a wall bracket.

Even those people who live in towns and have only a balcony or window ledge of a flat or bed-sitter to attract feeding birds can get a lot of enjoyment from putting up a hanging bird table which can be attached to a wall by a strong bracket.

There are also many types of food baskets and tit feeders which can be hung close to the window of a flat or town apartment.

Chapter Five

Some Birds to Look for, Feed and Encourage to Nest in the Garden

In this chapter I have selected, and briefly described, 40 species which you may see at different times of the year. Some are resident all the time, and common; others are migrants and stay only for a short period in summer or winter. A few of these garden birds are shy and only occasionally venture near the house, but there is a good chance you will see most of them after a few seasons of careful watching and attracting them by putting out food and providing nest boxes. The illustrations which accompany my species notes should also prove helpful in identifying visitors to your garden.

LIFESPAN OF BIRDS

The average life expectancy of wild birds is short and subject to variation according to species and habitat. The following list of the maximum recorded lifespans of some birds is based on information obtained from ringing. If you find a bird with a ring on its leg, make a note of its number and send full details of date, place, species, whether it was alive or dead, and any other data, to the British Trust for Ornithology (see page 94). You will be informed when and where the bird was ringed. If you find a racing pigeon with a numbered ring, send details to the Royal Pigeon Racing Association (see page 94). They do not register all pigeons, but would be able to supply details of other relevant organisations to contact.

Blackbird	10 years
Blackcap	5
Bullfinch	8
Chaffinch	10
Dunnock	8
Fieldfare	5
Goldcrest	3
Goldfinch	8
Greenfinch	13
Gull (Black-headed)	30
Hawfinch	3
Jackdaw	14
Jay	18
Magpie	15
Martin (House)	6
Nuthatch	9
Owl, Tawny	17
Pigeon, Wood	14
Robin	11
Starling	20
Sparrow, House	11
Sparrow, Tree	10
Swallow	16
Spotted Flycatcher	8
Thrush, Song	14
Thrush, Mistle	10
Tit, Blue	11
Tit, Coal	6
Tit, Great	10
Tit, Long-tailed	4
Tit, Marsh	10
Wagtail, Pied	7
Woodpecker, Green	5
Woodpecker, Great Spotted	9
Wren	5

Wood Pigeon

(Columba palumbus) : Length 41 cm (16 in.)

The largest and commonest pigeon, also known as the ring dove because of the white ring on its neck. Look for the white bars on its wings and dark bar on the tail. Its wings make a noisy clatter when it takes off. This is not a popular visitor to the garden as it will greedily eat green crops such as cabbage, brussels sprouts and kale, particularly in hard winter weather.

It comes to garden feeding stations and is fond of grain and larger seeds. Although mainly a ground feeder, the wood pigeon occasionally visits bird tables for bread, household scraps and seeds. In summer it raids rows of garden peas.

Collared Dove

(Streptopelia decaocto) : Length 32 cm (12½ in.)

This attractive dove first arrived in Britain in 1954, after spreading across the Continent from Asia, and is now common. It often feeds in chicken runs and regularly comes to bird tables and ground-feeding stations for seeds, grain, peas and scraps. It also likes young foliage and berries. Look for its ash-brown plumage, with black half collar edged with white, and its dark wing tips. It likes perching on TV aerials where it sings with a treble-noted 'coo' which has the accent on the third syllable. It nests in coniferous trees and raises several broods.

Tawny Owl

(Strix aluco) : Length 38 cm (15 in.)

Also known as the brown owl or wood owl, this beneficial bird hunts for rodents in large gardens, parks and woods. It is not uncommon in the centre of some towns and villages. As well as eating rats and mice it also feeds on small birds, insects, worms and even frogs and newts. It can be attracted into gardens with large mature trees by putting up an enclosed, chimney-type nest box with a 20 cm (8 in.) diameter hole at the top and inside depth of 76 cm (30 in.). The floor should be 20 cm (8 in.) square. Tawny owls will also nest in old wooden barrels if holes are cut in them and the barrels are placed in tree crotches well above the ground.

Green Woodpecker

(Picus viridis) : Length 32 cm (12½ in.)

This woodland bird will come into gardens to feed on the ants' nests in lawns, picking up the ants and their pupae with its long, sticky tongue. It likes to search for insect larvae in tree trunks and branches, pressing against the surface with its stiff tail and using its zygodactyl feet (two toes pointing forward, two backward). It visits bird tables in winter for bird pudding, mealworms and fat. Nesting in gardens with large trees can be encouraged by putting up an enclosed-type nest box with a 6.5 cm (2½ in.) entrance hole and a depth of 38 cm (15 in.). Normally the green woodpecker bores its own nest hole in old trees.

Great Spotted Woodpecker

(Dendrocopos major) : Length 23 cm (9 in.)

The great spotted woodpecker is found in large gardens with well-grown trees as well as in woods and parks. It hammers trees and dead wood for insects and larvae with its strong, sharp bill and wedges nuts in crevices to crack them open. You can attract it to bird tables by putting out suet, fat and nuts. It is as agile as tits in hanging upside down on a piece of suet. As well as excavating its own nest hole in a tree it will use an enclosed-type nest box with a 5 cm (2 in.) entry hole and an interior depth of 30 cm (12 in.). Male has red on back of head but female has a black crown. Young of both sexes have completely red crowns.

Swallow

(Hirundo rustica) : Length 19 cm (7½ in.)

A summer visitor to house and garden which spends the winter in southern Africa, the swallow builds an open, cup-shaped mud nest on beams and ledges or against walls. It often chooses porches and out-houses in which to rear its young, and there are usually two broods. You can encourage swallows to nest by putting up a shallow wooden tray, or half a coconut, on a joist or rafter. They will also use the artificial nests made for house martins if these are specially adapted and put up singly inside buildings. Swallows catch insects on the wing, from ground level to as high as 150 metres (500 feet).

House Martin

(Delichon urbica) : Length 12.5 cm (5 in.)

A summer visitor, the house martin nests in groups under roofs and the eaves of houses. Two, sometimes three, broods are reared in mud cup nests. It differs from the swallow in having a white rump patch which contrasts with its blue-black upperparts and white underparts. Its tail is not as deeply forked as the swallow's and the swallow has a chestnut red forehead and throat. If you want to attract house martins put up artificial nests (see Chapter 3) under eaves or high window sills. House martins eat large numbers of flying insects and for this reason you should make a special effort to encourage them to nest.

Jackdaw

(Corvus monedula) : Length 33 cm (13 in.)

A small member of the crow family and the only black bird with a grey nape and ear coverts. It lives in groups and frequently comes into gardens. It is attracted to bird tables where it eats scraps, cold potatoes, fruit, berries and nuts. Mixed scraps put down on the ground are also eaten. In spring jackdaws can be a menace because they eat the eggs and young of other birds, and they build stick nests in chimneys, sometimes blocking them. If you want to have nesting jackdaws in the garden you can put up open- and enclosed-type nest boxes. The enclosed type should have an entry hole of not less than 15 cm (6 in.).

Magpie

(Pica pica) : Length 46 cm (18 in.)

This large and long-tailed piebald bird hunts on the ground and in hedges for small animals, birds and insects and it is also fond of fruit, nuts, peas and berries. It raids the nests of garden birds to take and eat eggs and young. In autumn and winter it will visit bird tables or garden ground-feeding stations for household scraps which it usually takes away to eat. Magpies will also attack the tops of milk bottles to get at the cream. Like the jackdaw this is a fierce predator on other birds so it is not always welcome in the garden.

Jay

(Garrulus glandarius) : Length 34 cm (13½ in.)

If you have a large garden with plenty of trees you are certain to receive a visit from jays. They are fond of acorns, which they bury for winter food, and they come to bird tables and ground-feeding areas for household scraps, cold potatoes, corn, beechmast, nuts, fruit and berries. Don't encourage too many visits from jays as they are serious predators of eggs and young birds in the garden. They are particularly partial to green peas, which puts them on the gardener's 'black list'. Look for the white rump and bright blue and black wing patches which show up in flight.

Great Tit

(Parus major) : Length 14 cm (5½ in.)

The great tit is one of our commonest garden birds and a very frequent visitor to bird tables and hanging nut containers. It spends a lot of time feeding on or near the ground and likes to peck through the foil of milk bottles to get at the cream. An acrobatic species which delights you with its antics as it hangs on halved coconuts, pieces of fat and suet, peanut baskets and bags containing scraps. You can encourage it to nest by putting up an enclosed-type of nest box with a 2.75 cm (1⅛ in.) diameter entry hole and an interior depth of at least 12.5 cm (5 in.). It naturally nests in tree holes or wall cavities, and sometimes chooses letter-boxes.

Blue Tit

(Parus caeruleus) : Length 11.5 cm (4½ in.)

You can encourage this, and all other tit species, by hanging up baskets of nuts, scraps and fat, halved coconuts and pieces of suet and fat. Like the great tit it raids milk bottles on doorsteps for the cream. An adaptable bird, it nests in tree holes, wall cavities, drainpipes, letter-boxes, even car dashboards. It likes to build in the enclosed-type nest box with 2.5 cm (1 in.) to 2.75 cm (1⅛ in.) entry hole. Blue tits eat many garden insect pests but they damage buds and ripe fruit. The only small bird with mainly blue-and-yellow plumage.

Coal Tit

(Parus ater) : Length 11.5 cm (4½ in.)

This active little bird, which likes gardens and plantations where there are coniferous trees, does not visit the bird table as commonly as great tits and blue tits but likes to swing on peanut containers, chunks of fat and suet and halved coconuts. In winter it is often seen foraging for spiders and insects with other tit species. Look for the white spot on the back of the blue-black head. Its small size is also distinctive. It nests in tree holes and wall cavities but will use the same type of nest box as the blue tit. Usually single-brooded, it has seven to eleven young.

Marsh Tit

(Parus palustris) : Length 11.5 cm (4½ in.)

A woodland bird which is often seen in gardens, its popular name is misleading as it is not usually seen in marshes. Look for its glossy black cap and chin patch, white cheeks and grey back. It hunts in gardens for insects and you can attract it to the bird table and hanging containers by putting out a plentiful supply of fat and nuts. It nests in tree and wall holes and often rears two broods. It chooses enclosed-type nest boxes like other tits and you may be lucky enough to have a nesting pair using a hole in an old tree.

Long-tailed Tit

(Aegithalos caudatus) : Length 14 cm (5½ in.)

A pretty little black, white and pink bird with very long tail, it is really an inhabitant of woodland and scrub but sometimes enters gardens in winter with mixed flocks of tits and goldcrests. In the coldest weather it comes to bird tables and containers of fat and nuts. It has been reported more frequently from gardens in recent years as natural cover in the countryside is destroyed by farming operations. Occasionally in larger gardens with a wild patch of scrub and brambles, a pair will stay to nest. The beautiful, domed structure is made of cobwebs and mosses lined with thousands of feathers.

Nuthatch

(Sitta europaea) : Length 14 cm (5½ in.)

A tree-climbing woodland bird with a powerful, pointed bill like that of a woodpecker, it often moves head downwards on tree trunks or branches. A favourite visitor to bird tables and containers of nuts and fat because of its quick and acrobatic habits. It wedges nuts and acorns in crevices and batters them open. Put out sunflower seeds, peanuts, fat and cake for it on the bird table. It normally nests in a tree hole but you can sometimes encourage it to occupy an enclosed-type nest box. The female reduces the entry hole to the right size with mud.

Tree Creeper

(Certhia familiaris) : Length 12.7 cm (5 in.)

This brown and white woodland bird creeps up trees and branches in a mouse-like way, moving in a series of jerks and pressing its stiff tail against the bark. If you have a Wellingtonia tree in the garden you are likely to find a tree creeper roosting in an egg-shaped hollow which it has excavated in the soft bark with its long bill. It does not come to bird tables but you can attract it by putting crushed nuts and porridge in tree crevices. It sometimes uses a conventional enclosed-type nest box but it prefers a special wedge-shaped box or a piece of bark or cork nailed to a tree (see Chapter 3).

Wren

(Troglodytes troglodytes) : Length 9.5 cm (3¾ in.)

The smallest brown bird in the garden, the wren is now common again after sustaining heavy losses during the great freeze-up in the winter of 1962-3. It likes the cover of shrubberies and ivy-covered walls, where it creeps about in search of insects and spiders. It is not a visitor to feeding stations but you can encourage it in the garden by putting up an enclosed-type nest box in which it builds its domed nest. It will also use holes in trees, buildings and banks and old sacking (see Chapter 3). It is one of the best songsters, with a loud and vibrant trill.

Mistle Thrush

(Turdus viscivorus) : Length 27 cm (10½ in.)

The largest British thrush, it is so named because of its fondness for mistletoe berries. It is a more upright bird than the song thrush and has a distinctive, dipping flight during which it makes a churring call. It can be attracted to bird tables in hard weather by a supply of sultanas and bird pudding. You should also put out old apples on the ground as it finds these irresistible. Mistle thrushes are fond of berries, particularly cotoneaster and hawthorn. If you have tall old trees with ivy clumps you may encourage it to nest in a fork, or along a branch, early in spring.

Fieldfare

(Turdus pilaris) : Length 25.5 cm (10 in.)

A winter visitor to the garden from Scandinavia, the fieldfare flies like a mistle thrush but has a chuckling, 'chack-chack' call. It comes into the garden to eat berries on shrubs and trees and also likes old apples put down on the ground in frosty and snowy weather. It comes to bird tables for scraps, fruit and berries. If possible leave some apples on your trees in autumn to encourage flocks of fieldfares into the garden from the open fields.

Song Thrush

(Turdus philomelos) : Length 22.8 cm (9 in.)

A friend of the gardener, destroying many pests, it eats snails and smashes open the shells on stones or paving slabs. It likes to feed on the ground but is rather nervous and wary. It eats household scraps, fruit and cheese and is particularly fond of sultanas. Like the other thrushes it loves old apples and berries. It nests in bushes, ivy clumps and sometimes the ledges of buildings. One of the finest of our garden songsters, with repeated musical phrases.

Redwing

(Turdus iliacus) : Length 21 cm (8¼ in.)

Like the fieldfare, this is a winter visitor from Norway and Sweden. It is a small and delicate thrush which cannot endure long cold spells. It comes into the garden to feed on berries and snails and large flocks can be seen in grassy fields as they search for worms. It will come to ground-feeding stations for berries, seeds, scraps and old apples and is particularly fond of hawthorn berries. Look for its distinctive, chestnut-red flank patches and bold white eyestripe.

Blackbird

(Turdus merula) : Length 25 cm (10 in.)

A very common garden bird all the year round, it feeds in the open and in undergrowth but never strays far from cover of bushes and shrubs. A frequent visitor to the bird table and ground-feeding stations where it likes to eat fat, seeds, bird pudding, apples, cheese, sultanas and household scraps. The blackbird's beautiful fluted song and rattling alarm call are the most familiar sounds of the bird garden. It nests in hedges, evergreen bushes, ivy clumps and ledges of out-houses. It will also use a nest tray or an open-fronted type of nest box.

Robin

(Erithacus rubecula) : Length 14 cm (5½ in.)

Britain's most popular garden bird because of its jaunty habits and tameness, the robin often follows the gardener to get worms and grubs turned up by the spade. You can attract some robins to eat from the hand if you offer a regular supply of mealworms which they find irresistible. In winter the robin is a regular and quite aggressive visitor to the bird table, often chasing off birds of much greater size and weight. It eats nuts, seeds, oats, bird pudding, biscuit and breadcrumbs and household scraps. It naturally nests in tree and wall holes or thick ivy but can be attracted to build if you put out old kettles and cans (see Chapter 3) and tray-type or open-fronted wooden nest boxes.

Siskin

(Carduelis spinus) : Length 12 cm (4¾ in.)

This delightful little green-and-yellow and darkly-streaked finch has only started coming to gardens for food in recent winters. It is particularly attracted to peanuts hung up in red nylon-mesh bags but no-one knows exactly why it is so fond of the red colour. In winter it flocks with redpolls and feeds on the seeds of silver birch and alder, clinging acrobatically to the tiny cones. In summer it disperses to nest in northern coniferous woodland. It will sometimes come to bird tables for seed and nuts.

Goldcrest

(Regulus regulus) : Length 9 cm (3½ in.)

Britain's tiniest bird, weighing a mere five grammes, it likes gardens and woods where there are coniferous and evergreen trees, spending much of its time flitting among the branches or searching bark for insects, spiders and larvae. Easily told by its small size, dull green back and orange-yellow crest bordered with black. It mixes with flocks of tits and treecreepers in winter. It is very tame and comes to bird tables to peck at fat or to eat small crumbs. Highly acrobatic, it often hangs upside down. Its nest is an intricately-woven hammock of spiders' webs and moss hung from a branch of a coniferous tree.

Spotted Flycatcher

(Muscicapa striata) : Length 14 cm (5½ in.)

A summer visitor from Africa, this dull-looking bird is a wonderful flier, dashing out from a perch to snap up passing insects as large as dragonflies and butterflies. It nests against walls, tree trunks or in holes of trees and walls. You can encourage it to nest by putting up an open-fronted wooden nest box, but take care to see it is in a protected site not accessible to marauding cats. Spotted flycatchers like wooden posts or dead branches from which to make their insect-catching flights and you can put up a post with crosspiece for them.

Dunnock

(Prunella modularis) : Length 14.5 cm (5¾ in.)

A common and drab-coloured garden bird which spends much of its time on the ground or in low vegetation, moving forward with short jerks or a curious shuffling walk, frequently flicking its wings. In autumn and winter it comes to ground-feeding stations for crumbs, cake and seeds but is not a frequent visitor to the bird table. The dunnock, also known as the hedge sparrow, has a lively warbling song delivered in jerky bursts. It nests in hedges and evergreen bushes but you can often encourage it to nest by leaving a bunch of pea sticks or faggots against a fence or wall.

Pied Wagtail

(Motacilla alba) : Length 18 cm (7 in.)

The only small black and white British bird with a long tail, it often runs about on garden lawns picking up insects and bobbing its tail up and down. It is also known as the dish-washer as it paddles in shallow water, including garden pools, to feed on flies and gnats. It sometimes comes to garden-feeding stations in winter for crumbs and household scraps. It nests in holes in walls, thatch and creepers and will occupy a ledge-type or open-fronted wooden nest box which must be fixed to a wall or placed in a cavity that is safe from prowling cats.

Starling

(Sturnus vulgaris) : Length 21.5 cm (8½ in.)

One of our commonest birds, the large winter flocks include immigrants from the Continent. An aggressive feeder which pushes other birds away from the bird table or ground-feeding places. But it cannot compete so well on hanging containers and is always wary of human movement in the garden or at house windows. It nests in holes of trees and walls and in drainpipes. If the wood of a nest box is soft it will enlarge the entry holes of smaller birds such as tits. It eats almost all the food offered in the garden, being specially fond of household scraps, but also helps the gardener by eating many grubs and pests.

Hawfinch

(Coccothraustes coccothraustes) : Length 18 cm (7 in.)

A shy bird which is normally found in woods and parks or old orchards but sometimes comes into gardens. It is a wary visitor to the bird table for nuts, fruits and seeds. It has a massive bill which it uses to crack open cherry and plum stones to get at the kernels. In summer it comes into the garden to eat garden peas. Easily identified by top-heavy look, accentuated by its short tail, it nests on horizontal boughs of fruit trees. You can encourage it into the garden by planting cherry and plum trees or hornbeam trees. It is fond of the winged seeds of hornbeam.

Greenfinch

(Carduelis chloris) : Length 14.5 cm (5¾ in.)

A common and increasing garden bird which adores peanuts and is often the dominant bird at hanging nut containers. It comes to bird tables for all kinds of seeds, buckwheat and shelled nuts. The male greenfinch is a handsome bird with his olive-green plumage and bright yellow flashes on wings and tail; his mate is greyer and duller. Greenfinches are sociable and nest in groups of two to six pairs. The male makes bat-like song flights with slowly-flapping wings. If you have a rose hedge or bushes, greenfinches will come to eat the hips in winter.

Reed Bunting

(Emberiza schoeniclus) : Length 15 cm (6 in.)

Like its cousin, the yellowhammer (or yellow bunting) the reed bunting is an increasing visitor to gardens in winter. It normally lives in marshy and reedy places, but moves into suburban areas when the weather becomes hard in seach of mixed seeds and crumbs put out on bird tables. The male reed bunting is also known as the 'reed sparrow' because of its brown back and dark head markings. Its black head contrasts with a white moustache streak. Females and young birds are brown and lack the black head markings.

Goldfinch

(Carduelis carduelis) : Length 12 cm (4¾ in.)

This beautiful bird has a song which is as bright as its colouring. It commonly enters gardens to eat seeds and to nest in fruit trees, hedges and evergreen bushes. It will come to bird tables for mixed seeds, but it prefers to forage for the seeds in garden plants and weeds. Leave some of your garden bedding and border plants, such as gaillardia, cosmos and french marigold, as goldfinches like to feed on the seed heads in autumn. The goldfinch's elegant cup-shaped nest of mosses, grasses and lichens is often built in garden fruit trees or espalier bushes trained against walls.

Bullfinch

(Pyrrhula pyrrhula) : Length 16 cm (6¼ in.)

If you are a keen gardener you will view this handsome bird with very mixed feelings. It eats many buds of fruit trees and ornamental shrubs and is killed in large numbers by commercial fruit growers because of this damaging habit. But the bullfinch makes up for its bad ways by eating lots of weed seeds, including nettle and dock. It occasionally visits bird tables for seeds but prefers to forage for wild and garden seeds and berries. It is particularly fond of blackberries, privet berries and honeysuckle berries. It nests in thick evergreens and hedges.

Chaffinch

(Fringilla coelebs) : Length 15 cm (6 in.)

The commonest British finch which comes regularly to bird tables and ground-feeding stations. It likes all kinds of seeds, bird pudding, scraps and berries. If you have well-grown beech trees in the garden look for flocks of chaffinches feeding on fallen beech mast (nuts). Our birds are joined in winter by flocks from the Continent. It nests in old fruit trees, hedges and wall shrubs. The nest is one of the most beautiful built by a British bird. Lichens, grass and spiders' webs are used in its construction.

Brambling

(Fringilla montifringilla) : Length 14.5 cm (5¾ in.)

A close relative of the chaffinch, the brambling comes to Britain in winter from Scandinavia. In cold weather it visits garden bird tables with chaffinches for mixed seeds and is particularly fond of buckwheat, hemp and millet. It feeds in the wild on beech mast and should be looked for wherever there are a lot of these triangular seeds scattered on the ground. Look for the male brambling's orange-buff breast and shoulders. The female is duller, but both sexes have conspicuous white rumps. They call with a harsh 'dwee' note, rather like that of the greenfinch.

House Sparrow

(Passer domesticus) : Length 14.5 cm (5¾ in.)

This common and gregarious bird, which benefits so much from living close to man, can be a menace on the bird table and at ground-feeding stations. It crowds out less robust species by sheer energy and force of numbers. House sparrows are also aggressive usurpers of nest boxes and house martins' nests. The only way to deal with them when they become a nuisance is to destroy their nests as these are built. Sparrows make up for their bad ways to some extent by their chirpy and adaptable ways and their consumption of insects and weed seeds, though gardeners find it hard to forgive their destruction of crocuses and other spring flowers.

Tree Sparrow

(Passer montanus) : Length 14 cm (5½ in.)

Shyer than the house sparrow, the tree sparrow does come to bird tables for household scraps and seeds, though it is usually no match for the overbearing house sparrow. You can attract tree sparrows into the garden by putting up enclosed-type nest boxes with 2.75 cm (1⅛ in.) diameter entry holes. They like old trees with holes in the trunks, ivy clumps and thatched roofs for nesting and will join a mixed flock of finches and buntings to feed on corn, seeds and scraps put down on the ground in the garden. Look for the chocolate-brown crown (the top of the house sparrow's head is grey), black spot on white cheek, and double white wing bar. The voice is more musical and metallic than that of the house sparrow.

Blackcap

(Sylvia atricapilla) : Length 14 cm (5½ in.)

This warbler is a summer visitor to the garden from Africa but some winter in Britain and are often seen at bird tables. You can tell the male from the female by his glossy cap; his mate has a reddish-brown crown. The blackcap keeps well hidden for most of the time but in autumn and winter ventures out to feed on crumbs, scraps, rolled oats and berries on the bird table and the glossy red berries of honeysuckle. It eats large quantities of harmful insects. A fine singer, considered by some to be second only to the nightingale.

Chapter Six

Welcoming the Birds that Visit Your Garden

When you set out to attract birds to your garden there are four basic points to meet. You must supply the right kind of foods in correct season as well as a regular water supply. There must also be plenty of shelter, from weather and enemies, in which to roost and nest and there must be freedom from persecution and predation.

In this chapter I show how these points can be achieved without much cost. The aim is to attract birds to your garden and home area and the initial outlay on equipment and suitable trees, shrubs and plants will quickly bring its own rewards and pleasures.

You should remember that a garden which attracts a wide range of bird life also has its own special problems. You must take precautions against attacks by your feathered neighbours on fruit, seedlings, salad and green crops. Blackbirds find strawberries and other soft fruit irresistible and they will take their share of your cherries. House sparrows, wood pigeons, skylarks and other birds play havoc with tender greenery. Sparrows are particularly troublesome in spring when they peck at crocuses and polyanthus blooms. The money you will need to spend on netting and black cotton to keep the birds off your most valued crops and flower beds is a small price to·pay for the many hours of pleasure you get from watching and listening to garden birds.

Bullfinches are among the most colourful birds in the garden, but they are as much a problem to the gardener as they are to the professional fruit grower. In winter and early spring they eat the buds of many fruit trees, lilac and forsythia. The worst bullfinch raids on fruit buds follow those autumns when their natural foods, such as the seeds (mast) of ash trees, are in short supply. You can't always be on the alert to scare marauding bullfinches away from your trees and shrubs. The most effective remedy I can recommend is a cobwebby material available from garden centres which I drape over the branches. This substance makes the fruit trees look unsightly during the vulnerable period in my garden, but it certainly works as an effective deterrent.

Jays and magpies are other unwelcome callers. They steal fruit and green peas and raid nests, eating both eggs and young birds. I am afraid there is little you can do to prevent these bold and greedy members of the crow family from raiding the garden. I suppose it is some compensation that both species have such handsome plumage. I particularly admire the bright blue and black wing flashes of the jay. When I was a boy growing up in an Essex village, the best Sunday hats of my father and all his farming friends were adorned with bunches of these bright feathers – evidence that many jays had paid the ultimate price of their sorties into the rows of green peas in local gardens and allotments.

When you are considering the profit-and-loss account of birds in your garden sanctuary, remember that even common and obtrusive birds like the house sparrow and starling eat their share of insects which are garden pests. On balance, the presence of birds is beneficial to a well-organised garden and there is the welcome bonus of their colour and vivacity to enhance the beauty of your trees, shrubs, flowers and lawns.

Adaptable creatures like birds are certainly not discouraged by built-up areas. If you provide their basic requirements they will feed and nest close to the house. Many of the commoner birds adapted their lives to our gardens after their original woodland and hedgerow homes had been either destroyed or modified through human activities. They then found that the closeness of man protected them from such natural enemies as the fox, weasel, stoat and wild cat on the ground, and birds of prey, magpies and crows in the air. Swallows, house martins, house sparrows and starlings found human dwellings gave them plenty of places in which to nest and rear their young.

Some readers may be without a garden, or unable to go out of doors because of illness or infirmity. They can still derive lots of enjoyment from a bird-feeding station on a window sill. One of my friends is a retired Army officer, now almost completely bedridden through illness, who keeps cheerful and busy watching birds. He has clamped a bird table to a wide window sill outside his bedroom and hangs from it a variety of wire or nylon containers and baskets containing nuts and household scraps.

My friend has already listed some uncommon species. As well as blue tits, great tits, coal tits and greenfinches, the regular visitors, his greatest triumph so far has been to attract some siskins, pretty green and yellow finches, to his red nylon peanut bags. These little birds, winter visitors from northern Britain, clung acrobatically to the bags as they pecked at the nuts through the mesh.

Before I examine the best ways to attract birds to your garden, I should deal with the important subject of binoculars and telescopes. You will want to watch and study the birds from your house, or a part of the garden offering concealment, so that you don't disturb your subjects. If your bird table and feeding containers are properly positioned so as to give clear and reasonably close views from the house you will certainly not need the help of the high-powered optical aids used by birdwatchers in open country or by seashore and estuary.

There are three main optical points to consider when making your choice of binoculars: magnification, field of view (usually measured in degrees, or in yards width at 1,000 yards distance), and light transmission. For general birdwatching, magnifications of x 7, x

8 or x 9, with object lenses of 30 millimetres and 40 millimetres diameter, are the most suitable. I use a pair of Zeiss Jena Jenopten 8 x 30 binoculars for my own garden birdwatching and a pair of 10 magnification Zeiss Dekarem for field work. There is a bewildering choice of binoculars on the market to suit all pockets but buy the best you can afford. I also use a Japanese-made telescope with a fixed magnification of x 22 for looking at birds which visit my bird tables and feeders. This particular model is compact and light and can be used without a tripod. You focus by turning a knob which is a great improvement on older models where you had to push draw-tubes in and out.

Buy the best binoculars you can afford for watching your birds.

One of the great attractions of some garden birds is their tameness. However, you should bear in mind that birds like the jackdaw and starling, which quickly lose their fear of humans when offered food, can take most of the supplies you provide for shyer species. Robins are easy to tame and delightful to have near, or even in, the house, but a tame robin is often more aggressive than one which is treated like the other birds in the garden. He tends to be lord of the bird table or window sill. If you train a robin to take food from your hand, it is better to do it on the opposite side of the house from the bird table.

I am often asked to define the best kind of bird garden and miniature sanctuary. The truth is that the ideal bird sanctuary would hardly be a garden, in the true sense of the word, but rather a mixture of trees, shrubs and flowers with a good supply of weeds and tangled, jungle corners. There would be nettle beds, brambles, old tree stumps and old tin cans and kettles on the ground and in forks of trees in which robins and wrens could build their nests.

Naturally this sort of layout does not appeal to the tidy person who wants a neat, well-ordered flower, shrub and vegetable garden. If you are to have the best of both worlds you must aim for a compromise, particularly if your garden is a small one.

If you have room at the end of the garden for a patch of rough grass, brambles and nettles, or a wild area under trees, then include it in your plan. A nettle bed not only provides an area where small birds can search for insects, and low cover where some species like the whitethroat can build nests. It is also the feeding place for the caterpillars of the peacock, small tortoise-shell and red admiral butterflies.

The bird garden should be built with a variety of levels which give birds shelter and areas where they can safely feed. When I made my present garden around a new house, one of my first jobs was to build a low stone wall which could be viewed from one of the large picture windows. The raised bed, covered with low-growing shrubs and plants, is a happy hunting ground for birds at all seasons of the year and doesn't get snowed up in winter. Song thrushes and blackbirds love to prod for food among the plants which trail over the wall. The thrushes find snails under the leaves and use some of the flat stones as anvils to break them open.

Different levels in the garden provide shelter and feeding places.

Keep bushes and shrubs pruned for bushy growth to encourage nesting birds.

One of the reasons why Britain has such a large population of song birds compared with other countries is its profusion of hedges, spinneys and small tracts of open, mixed woodland. Many hedges are rapidly being bulldozed on farmland to make fields bigger and to make it easier to use the large machines which are part and parcel of modern agricultural practice. This is a regrettable trend but if you remember that old farm hedges represent a vital habitat for birds you will have a personal incentive to redress the balance by creating your own hedges and banks.

In my first garden I planted a hawthorn hedge which grew quickly and provided nest sites for blackbirds, song thrushes, whitethroats, wrens, dunnocks, greenfinches and linnets. A boundary hedge of this type also offers winter shelter and food. Thrushes, blackbirds, redwings and fieldfares eat the hawthorn berries and small birds like tits, wrens and dunnocks forage among the leaves and natural litter along the hedge bottom for insects, larvae, woodlice and centipedes.

Near my home an enterprising water company has planted a long holly hedge, always kept neatly trimmed, round its pumping station and the houses of employees. This smart hedge is a paradise for nesting birds as well as being a much-admired feature of the landscape.

To make your own garden a true sanctuary where a number of bird species will nest and migrants can find cover and food you must ensure that trees and shrubs are not allowed to get too lanky. As a general rule most bushes and shrubs are best for birds when they are trimmed and pruned to give bushy growth. Aim to keep trees at a medium height, say three to four metres, but all pruning must take into account the type of tree and its growth rate.

Chapter Seven

Planning and Planting a Garden that will Attract Birds

In earlier chapters I have given some information on trees, shrubs and flowering plants suitable for the garden bird sanctuary; we can now take a more detailed look at them.

While many gardeners will be modifying an established layout, some will be starting from scratch. Naturally, it is impossible to suggest a scheme to fit all requirements. Gardens come in so many different shapes and sizes, with so many types of soil, that I can only give a set of guidelines and leave the individual to work out the best plan according to local conditions and the amount of money in the kitty for planting.

As I pointed out earlier, there must be a compromise between the practical needs of the gardener and the requirements of a small sanctuary. Your main aim is to provide the basic essentials. On one side of the garden you will certainly need a hedge to provide cover and nest sites, and on another a row or groups of fast-growing, leafy shrubs with plenty of branching wood for perches and nests. You will then make sure that young birds in the nests have concealment from enemies and shelter from hot sun and rain.

If you study the winds which prevail in your home area, you will be able to work out the best planting programme to give birds cover. As my garden is in a high position exposed to northerly and easterly winds, I have made sure that my evergreen hedges cut off the worst of the gusts from these quarters.

The other essentials, which must be stressed, are a variety of levels, provided by rockeries, say, or low stone walls; a lawn easily viewed from one of the main windows; perches and posts for birds like the spotted flycatcher which make particular use of such vantage points; a rustic archway for climbers such as honeysuckle and roses which produce edible berries, trellises for training berry-bearing evergreens, and a wild patch where brambles, nettles and other plants normally classed as weeds are allowed to grow. Don't let them get out of hand and invade the rest of the garden.

Though the key to all your planning is the welfare of the birds, careful selection and positioning of your plants will accentuate the beauty of flowers and foliage, so that your garden is a charming setting for your home life as well as for the birds. Whatever you plant, consider the effect from the main windows of the house – your principal observation point. There will be some secluded areas which are not visible from the house, of course, but you can usually place trees and shrubs so they can be seen from one or more windows.

In planting new trees select native rather than foreign species.

Few small gardens can support slow-growing forest trees like the oak, but if you have the space and patience, then by all means plant one. As it develops it will attract and support its own large community of birds and the insects on which they feed.

Faster-growing subjects are ash, birch and willow. A word of caution about willows and poplars (of all kinds): they are not suitable for planting near houses because their roots are bad for foundations. Many people have planted weeping willows close to houses only to regret it deeply afterwards. These trees have a phenomenal rate of growth and often have to be felled because they have spread much too close to house walls and block out light. If you must plant a willow – and it is of little value in the bird garden – then put it well away from the house and its foundations.

In my own garden I have a spendid silver birch, which is a feature of the front lawn and attracts many birds. Redpolls and siskins come to feed on its seeds in winter, and many other species use its spreading branches for perching and hunting for insects throughout the year.

When choosing trees and shrubs, pay attention to the ultimate texture provided by twigs, branches and leaves. Birds need to be able to move about freely inside bush cover, and a hen bird sitting on her nest must be able to slip away quickly, unhampered by too much thick growth if danger threatens.

Some gardeners make a fetish of closely-clipped low hedges. These may look wonderfully neat, but they leave no room for birds to manoeuvre and are usually shunned.

Thorny hedges and trees are favoured because of the protection they afford against all kinds of nest robber – human and animal. The foliage of a tree, shrub or hedge must give sufficient protection against extremes of weather as well as from predators. Pruning is necessary to encourage trees and hedges to form the maximum number of fork structures strong enough to support nests. Cut the branches so that each fork contains at least three branches. The fork should be at an angle of 70 degrees, facing vertically upwards.

We can now consider the best trees, shrubs and climbers for supplying a crop of berries, a major consideration in the planting of the garden. As garden centres sell most of these subjects container-grown, you can start your collection at any season except the bleak depths of winter.

Barberry *(Berberis)*   A large family of spiny bushes which bear red and orange berries for the birds. *B.stenophylla* and *B.darwinii* are evergreens which tend to grow lanky if not trimmed: they can be grown as hedges. *B.aggregata* carries plenty of berries and will reach a height of three metres. Barberry hedges offer good nest sites for blackbirds, thrushes and finches.

Blackberry   Valuable in its cultivated forms for training against a fence where you can leave some berries for the birds. Wild blackberry briars, if left in a rough corner of the garden, must be trimmed back. The dense cover is good for nests and roosts.

Cotoneaster   Invaluable family of shrubs for berries and leafy cover, the deciduous *Cotoneaster horizontalis* (the Fishbone Cotoneaster) and *C.rotundifolia* grow to more than a metre high; *C.horizontalis* is often trained against a wall and its berries attract flocks of waxwings when these handsome Scandinavian birds come to Britain in winter. *C.dammeri* and *C.prostrata* have a trailing habit. *C.buxifolia*, *C.lacteus* and *C.francheti* are evergreens which are suitable for placing against a wall or fence. *C.lacteus* forms a fine, tall hedge with arching habit and is thick with red berries in winter. Another good

82

hedge subject in the group is *C.simonsii*. No bird garden is effective without a selection of hardy, quick-growing cotoneasters.

Elder Looked on with disdain as a weed by some gardeners, but well worth including if you have enough space. Its hollow wood is brittle. It has a lank, open growth and needs pruning to provide the best effect. The fragrant white flowers and vivid purple berries are attractive; the berries are greedily gobbled by the thrush family, tits and warblers – and are much in demand among the brewers of home-made wine.

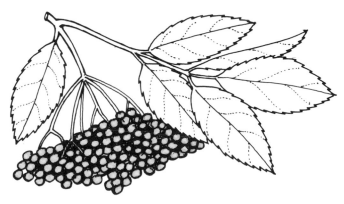

Hawthorn Can be clipped to form a thick hedge, proof against dogs or vandals and providing nest cover. Individual trees or hedges are good for berries and the varieties with red or pink flowers add rich colour to the garden scene.

Holly Another excellent choice for an evergreen hedge, though fairly slow growing. If you are planting bushes, you will need both a male and a female to ensure a crop of berries.

Honeysuckle Choose both evergreen and deciduous forms for your fences and trellises; also train honeysuckle against old tree stumps and posts. The cover is used for nests, and the berries are eaten by blackbirds, tits and warblers.

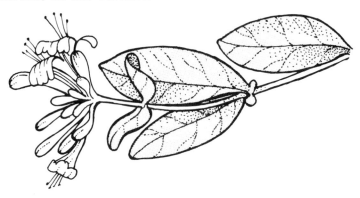

Ivy Although ivy has a bad reputation for strangling trees and destroying mortar, it is not nearly as bad as painted. It is valuable in the birds garden for its cover and for its berries. Ring the changes with variegated forms. Most types are good for covering unsightly stumps and mounds.

Rowan The mountain ash is a 'must' and makes a graceful feature tree in a lawn or garden corner. It carries a big crop of berries in August. If you have room, you can plant one or two of the other varieties, with pink or yellow berries, as well as the common rowan with its usual red and orange clusters. Brilliant russet leaf colours are an autumn bonus.

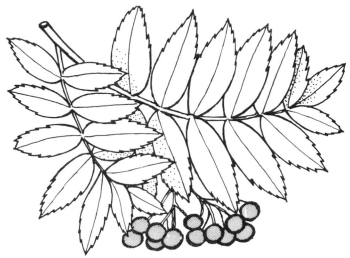

Spindle Worth growing for its pink and orange fruits; it prefers a chalky soil.

Viburnum This is a large family of shrubs. I grow the truly wild guelder rose, which has a crop of shiny, glutinous berries much loved by birds, and also the cultivated *Viburnum compactum*.

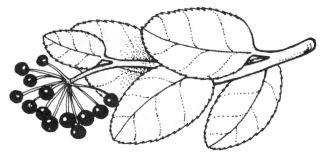

Yew This is a valuable evergreen which makes a good hedge and offers nest sites. It is slow growing and may take many years to produce berries.

Most of the usual shrubs which do well against walls are worth including. In addition to the berry-bearing shrubs I have listed, you can try escallonias, ceanothus, rambler roses, clematis and wistarias. Spotted flychatchers like old wistarias as nesting places.

Personally I am not all that fond of privet as a hedging subject but it offers both cover and purple berries which attract bullfinches. Laurel, as I have already mentioned, makes fine hedges if kept well trimmed and bushy and can hold many nests of blackbirds and thrushes.

Fruit trees are popular, particularly when fan-trained against a fence or wall. I get goldfinches, chaffinches and greenfinches nesting in mine.

In Chapter 2 I dealt with the need for a bird bath or pond. If you make a pond from concrete (not forgetting to seal it with a bituminous paint), or from a heavy gauge polythene lining, you will want to stock it with some oxygenating aquatic plants. The following will grow in a few centimetres of soil covered by shallow water:

Sagittaria graminea   *Eleocharis acicularis*
Isoetes lacustris (Quillwort)   *Hottonia palustris (Water Violet)*
Tillaea recurva   *Callitriche autumnalis.*

Birds are attracted to the insects, which come to the water plants, as well as to the water itself for drinking, bathing and preening.

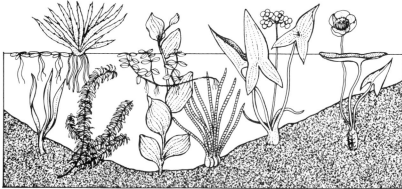

Oxygenating aquatic plants will keep a pond clear.

Chapter Eight

Predators, Pests and Poisons

No one who is serious about a garden bird sanctuary can be happy about cats prowling through the shrubberies and across the lawns. Let me say at once that I am not against cats. It so happens that our household pet has always been a dog, but I do like cats and I realise that many bird gardeners will want to keep one of these popular animals, hoping it will not take too heavy a toll of birds.

Nevertheless there is no escaping the fact that the cat is a ruthless and resourceful predator. That is its nature and nothing will change it – even the most domesticated cat will stalk and kill adult birds and their young. Before we consider the cat problem in more detail, a word about the bells which people put round their pets' necks, in the hope that birds will be warned by the noise and escape: the truth is that bells are, at best, only partly effective, though certainly better than nothing. They have a nasty habit of jamming or corroding so that they do not ring, and cats are adept at moving stealthily to reduce the sound.

It is the sight and presence of a cat in the garden which alarms birds and often makes them desert their nests. Even if your particular pet is not a persistent killer of birds, it does not really fit in with the bird garden, so that the best you can do is to minimise its effect on the bird population and deter neighbours' cats from entering to add to the difficulties.

Although it is not attractive, a wire fence offers some defence against marauding cats. Because my dog is a boisterous cat chaser, I don't have to worry unduly about the problem, but some of my neighbours have erected 5 cm mesh wire netting up to twelve metres high. They grow climbing plants like clematis, honeysuckle and *passiflora* (passion flower) up the netting. Thick, prickly hedges make good cat deterrents. Holly, hawthorn and sweet briar are excellent, but to make sure that cats and other undesirables do not find their way through, plug gaps with thorny cuttings. While cats can leap walls and fences two metres high, a length of wire netting about 50 cm wide along the top of a fence will stop them getting over or sitting on top. You can prevent cats from climbing small trees by putting a circle of wire round the trunk.

Rats are a menace. They can climb trees and hedges for eggs or nestlings, and surplus bird food left on the ground will attract them into the garden. You can either put down a safe poison or use traps. If you decide on traps, bait them with cheese, cake or apple and set them before dusk. Try not to leave them unexamined all night because of the risk of trapping other, harmless animals. The best poisons are Warfarin and Raticate. Put them in the middle of a section of old drainpipe, as this is not likely to be entered by other creatures.

Grey squirrels are spreading fast and make a terrible nuisance of themselves in gardens, eating large numbers of eggs and young birds. They even enlarge the entry holes of nest boxes to get at nestlings. Dogs help to chase squirrels away but the only really effective methods of control are trapping and shooting.

In some large gardens, foxes can be a problem. They are on the increase in suburban areas and are growing bolder in their raids on chickens, pet rabbits, birds' eggs and young birds. They also take food from dustbins. Since they are agile climbers, little short of an expensive, tall, fox-proof wire fence will keep them out at night. You can try putting out metal objects which make the animals suspicious, in the belief that they may be traps.

There is little you can do to stop raids by jays, magpies and crows. Although some exasperated gardeners shoot nest raiders as a last resort, most of us are resigned to the fact that they will take a share of eggs and young birds each spring.

Certain garden and agricultural pesticides and insecticides pose a threat to bird life, though in recent years special efforts have been made by manufacturers to produce chemicals which are non-toxic to birds and animals and not residual in the soil. Some of the harmful organo-chlorine substances are still in use, despite all the evidence against them, but you can make sure that none is used in your garden. Steer clear of DDT-based pesticides, and also slug baits containing metaldehyde. This chemical is a threat to hedgehogs and birds which eat contaminated slugs and snails. If you must use a slug bait, then ask for one containing Fertosan, which kills by contact and does not harm humans, birds, animals and earthworms.

In my garden, I use only pyrethrum-based insecticides containing a substance extracted from an African-grown flower and harmless to wildlife and humans, though effective against insect pests. When using a pyrethrum spray, confine your operations to the evening when bees are off the wing.

To sum up: never use insecticides containing aldrin, dieldrin, DDT and BHC. Always read the small print on tins and containers to make sure you know what you are buying. Better still, do not use any controls unless a pest is reaching epidemic scale – and then go for a product guaranteed harmless to birds and animals using the garden.

Chapter Nine

Projects for the Bird Gardener

When you have established your bird garden you will want to keep a permanent record of the resident and migratory species seen throughout the year. There are a number of simple projects which can widen your interest and enjoyment and add to the general store of natural history knowledge.

Every good birdwatcher keeps careful notes of what he sees and hears. The usual methods involve the use of notebooks, diaries and card indexes. Years ago, when I had fewer family and business commitments, I kept a diary-style field notebook, in which I noted my daily observations of birds and other wildlife, weather conditions and all other relevant details. This method still has a lot to commend it, particularly if you are retired and have plenty of time to write up your notes and to make sketches of birds seen in the garden. Busy people will probably find a card index easier to keep as a source of quick reference.

If you decide to keep a nature notebook or diary, the first essential is a book with a waterproof cover. If possible, get an unlined type because this is more useful for making sketches and diagrams.

The essential point of a nature diary or notebook is to be systematic. It is very easy to start out with a burst of enthusiasm, then get lazy or bored and stop writing. You needn't make it a chore – it should be an enjoyable hobby. Note the species and numbers of birds in the garden, their behaviour and feeding habits, call notes, songs and flight patterns. It helps if you can draw a quick sketch of a

Note down all the details of the birds in your garden in a notebook or card index.

particular bird or piece of behaviour. You can check it later against the plates and information in a standard field guide.

In recent years I have used a simple card index for my records. A supply of cards and a small box to house them are not expensive and take up little space. Make out a card for each species as observed. Put its popular name in the top left hand corner, followed by the scientific name in brackets. You can find these details in any reputable field guide. The scientific names are necessary because they are international. Our vernacular names are unfamiliar in other countries, and it helps your knowledge to memorize at least some of the Latin names.

Follow the same guidelines as in the nature notebook, but keep to a shortened formula as space is more limited. The value of a card index is ease of handling and speed of checking records. The index is alphabetical and you don't have to wade through pages of notes to find a particular fact.

As your knowledge grows, you may care to help with one or more of the schemes run by the British Trust for Ornithology. The Trust runs recording projects and censuses. The data written by amateur ornithologists on specially issued cards is analysed by computer, and the results are published. An example is the nest box information scheme. (If you write to the Trust, it will send membership details and full information.) Membership of the Royal Society for the Protection of Birds will also bring you information and

Good results can be obtained when taping bird songs on an ordinary recorder.

suggestions for individual projects in the garden. Write to the RSPB for details. Both organizations publish first-class magazines, and the RSPB makes fine colour films of bird life. (See page 94.)

Bird photography is increasingly popular although it is not at all a cheap hobby by the time you have bought a good camera, colour film, a tripod, telephoto lenses and other necessary equipment. Even so, the bird gardener has splendid opportunities to photograph birds drinking, bathing and feeding.

You can try to record the songs and calls of birds in your garden. Recordings of a very high quality need sophisticated and expensive equipment, such as a parabolic reflector, but it is surprising how good results often are with some of the standard and relatively inexpensive microphones and recorders. Magazines on recording often contain helpful articles for the beginner. You can also buy recorded bird song from the RSPB and some commercial companies which help you to identify and memorize the notes of your garden birds.

If you enjoy sketching and painting, then the garden is a good place to try your hand at bird art. Many of the greatest illustrators of natural history books began in this way. Watch the movements and postures of birds and try to capture these in preliminary sketches. Make careful notes, too, of how the natural colours strike you in changing lights. In my view the first notebook sketches of top bird artists like Archibald Thorburn are more charming and vivacious than many of his finished paintings. They contain the true essence of bird life.

Try your hand at painting or sketching your bird visitors.

Chapter Ten

Looking after Injured Birds

Everyone who attracts and feeds birds should become acquainted with the law as it relates to bird life. All birds and their eggs are protected under the Protection of Birds Act, 1954 (with amendments in 1967), except for game birds and certain scheduled pest species which may be killed or taken by authorised persons. Game birds and pests are listed in the schedule at the end of the Act. If you want to know more about the law affecting birds you should write to the RSPB, or you can contact your nearest police station or RSPCA Inspector. The RSPB publishes a useful booklet on *Birds and the Law* and will send a copy on receipt of a first-class stamp.

From time to time, you will come across an injured bird, or a fledgling which is orphaned or has prematurely left the nest. All too often, well-meaning people try to take over the care of young birds under the mistaken impression that they have been abandoned by their parents. In most cases, these youngsters are still being fed and should *not* be moved indoors.

If you decide to act as foster parent to a young bird which is definitely orphaned, make sure first of all that you have the necessary time and patience. If you don't, then it is far better to humanely destroy the little bird, or to hand it to someone more skilled at looking after it.

Only attempt to foster an orphaned bird if you have the necessary time and patience.

Young birds should be kept in a warm, draught-free place. They can be fed a mixture of dead flies, smooth (never hairy) caterpillars and minced raw meat from the end of a matchstick. Birds of prey need roughage such as dead mice and chicks complete with fur or feathers. Don't feed live food; kill insects beforehand. Regular feeds, about once an hour, are essential and you must also provide water. As the youngster grows and begins to exercise its wings, take it into the garden, show it live caterpillars and insects and encourage it to fend for itself. It should be independent in about a month.

Put exhausted or starved adult birds into a box lined with newspaper, keeping the top of the box dark so the bird doesn't fly up to the light and hurt itself. Provide a shallow bowl of water, food and a stick, placed low down, for a perch. Seed-eating birds should be offered a standard seed mixture. Insect-eating or omnivorous birds need insects, chopped worms, smooth caterpillars, finely-shredded meat and some of the proprietary insect food sold by pet shops. Never give exhausted birds alcohol. Leave a light on as the bird recovers, to encourage it to eat. When it is strong enough to fly, release it in the wild, but if its condition deteriorates, take it at once to an RSPCA clinic.

Take injured birds straight to the nearest vet, RSPCA or PDSA clinic, where they can be given expert attention.

A box lined with newspaper will provide a safe resting place for an injured bird.

Useful Addresses

The Royal Society for the Protection of Birds, Station Road, Sandy, Bedfordshire, SG19 1BH (0767 80551)
The leading organization for bird conservation. It owns and runs many reserves, arranges meetings and exhibitions, makes and shows colour films and publishes much illustrated literature including *Birds* (magazine issued free to members). Write for details.

Young Ornithologists' Club, RSPB, Station Road, Sandy, Bedfordshire, SG19 1BH (0767 80551)
The national club for young birdwatchers (ages 7 to 15). Quarterly magazine, *Bird Life.*

British Trust for Ornithology, Beech Grove, Tring, Hertfordshire, HP23 5NR (044 282 3461)
Senior scientific organization which most serious amateur birdwatchers join. Members can take part in field studies, censuses and other systematic work. Thrice yearly journals, *Bird Study* and *Ringing and Migration.* Lending library: many publications. Write for details.

International Council for Bird Preservation (British Section), British Museum (Natural History), Cromwell Road, London, SW7
Important organization which co-ordinates worldwide efforts at bird protection. Issues annual report, journal.

Royal Pigeon Racing Association, The Reddings, near Cheltenham, Gloucestershire, GL51 6RN (0452 713529)

Suppliers of garden bird equipment

RSPB (Address above)
Range of equipment.

Nerine Nurseries, Welland, near Malvern, Worcestershire, WR13 6LN (06846 2350)
House martin nest cups.

Jamie Wood Products, Cross Street, Polegate, East Sussex, BN26 6BN (03212 3813)
Bird tables, nest boxes and other equipment.

Scottish National Institution for the War Blinded, Linburn, Wilkieston by Kirknewton, Midlothian, EH27 8DU (031 333 1369/1334)
Nest boxes.

Index

Figures in bold refer to
illustrations.